To Sharon...

The Lord is ... down on you dur...
season. Allow His light to
shine through you, and you
will be blessed, indeed!!

Anthony R. Paige

To Sharon,

May the Lord rain down His Shalom on you during this Season. May the blessings pass through you and gave you Indeed!

Sincerely, Jorge

"… unto the going down of the same, the Lord's name is to be praised. Psalm 113.3" King James Version

Fifty-Two Weeks to Praise Our God

God Moments Devotional

ANTHONY R. PAIGE

WESTBOW
PRESS®
A DIVISION OF THOMAS NELSON
& ZONDERVAN

WestBow Press books may be ordered through booksellers or by contacting:

WestBow Press
A Division of Thomas Nelson & Zondervan
1663 Liberty Drive
Bloomington, IN 47403
www.westbowpress.com
1 (866) 928-1240

ISBN: 978-1-9736-0751-9 (sc)
ISBN: 978-1-9736-0750-2 (hc)
ISBN: 978-1-9736-0752-6 (e)

Library of Congress Control Number: 2017915832

Print information available on the last page.

WestBow Press rev. date: 11/30/2017

God Moments

Be still and know that I am God; I
will be exalted among the heathen,
I will be exalted in the earth.

—Psalm 46:10

There are so many blessings that we receive from the Lord, if we are willing to be still before Him.

Every time our Father allows us to catch a glimpse of His greatness, we need to capture those moments. I call each experience a God Moment. It is my desire to remember each encounter, recognize it as a blessing, and to record my God Moments in a journal. Each time I re-read my entries, I will be reminded of the greatness of my God. As I share my God Moments with others, may they too be reminded of the greatness of our God.

Each week I pray that you will record your encounters with God. Share your God Moments. Share them with family and friends. Allow your encounters to proclaim to everyone the good news about our God!

LET EVERYTHING THAT HATH BREATH PRAISE
THE LORD! PRAISE, YE, THE LORD.

I WAS GLAD WHEN THEY SAID UNTO ME, LET
US GO INTO THE HOUSE OF THE LORD!

Just what is a God Moment?
It's your encounter with the King!
Where He'll replace your sorrow
With a song of praise to sing.

What's the purpose of God Moments?
That's a question you might ask …
It's to give your all to Almighty God,
And in His glorious presence, bask!

May God be with you now and forever more, and may
you allow His presence to bring about those supernatural
changes in your life that you so desperately desire …

That is my prayer for you …
This is my prayer for me …
Your servant …

Anthony

Contents

Acknowledgments. 1

Introduction. 2

Week 1: In the Beginning with the End in Mind!. .8
Genesis 1:1–31

Week 2: Step Toward a Bright Tomorrow! 10
Deuteronomy 30:1–20

Week 3: You Will Never Walk Alone! 12
Joshua 1:1–18

Week 4: You Made It Through the Battle!. 14
Judges 15, 16

Week 5: God's Love is in the Making!. 16
Ruth 1, 2, 3, 4

Week 6: Faith Is Trusting God During Trials! 18
Job 1, 2, 3

Week 7: Faith Is Trusting God All the Time! 20
Job 42

Week 8: Sing a Song to the Lord, Your God!. 22
Psalm 27

Week 9: Look at God's Beauty All Around You!. .24
Psalm 19

Week 10: Whose Plans Will You Follow This week?. 26
Jeremiah 29

Week 11: Lord Jesus, Awaken Us from Sleep! 28
John 11

Week 12: What Do You Have to Show for Your "Show and Tell" to God? 30
Luke 19

Week 13: We Serve as God's Ambassadors! 32
Romans 8:1–39

Week 14: Remember, We Are Victorious in God! 36
2 Chronicles 19, 20

Week 15: Leave Your Troubles in Gethsemane! 38
Matthew 26

Week 16: Complete This Week's Task! 40
Exodus 17

Week 17: Come Holy Spirit! 42
John 14

Week 18: Jesus! Jesus! Lord Jesus! 44
Mark 15, 16

Week 19: Blessed Are You! 46
Matthew 5

Week 20: Expectations! 48
Luke 1

Week 21: But Why, Lord? 50
Isaiah 55

Week 22: Let the Peace of the Lord Fill Your Mind! 52
Psalm 133, 134

Week 23: You're Perfect in His Sight! 54
2 Corinthians 5

Week 24: This Week! 56
Luke 9

Week 25: The Seasons Are a – Turning! 58
Isaiah 60

Week 26: Lord, May I Never Become So Proud! .60
Proverbs 16

Week 27: We Praise You Because You're Good! .64
Matthew 19, 20

Week 28: I Didn't Know—But You Did! 66
Judges 4, 5

Week 29: Come Out and Just Be You! 68
Esther 2

Week 30: My Meat Is to Do Thy Will, Lord God! 70
John 4

Week 31: Your Next Assignment, "Go!" 72
Matthew 28:16–20

Week 32: God's Gift for Today! 74
Galatians 5:1–26

Week 33: Hallelujah! It's Time to Ascend!...........................76
1 Thessalonians 4, 5

Week 34: Learning How to Trust! 78
Romans 8:26–39

Week 35: Deny Ourselves and Follow Christ!........................80
Mark 8:1–38

Week 36: I Trust in You, Lord Jesus! 82
Proverbs 3

Week 37: Look Straight Ahead Unto Jesus!.........................84
Proverbs 4

Week 38: When You Are Weary, Come to Jesus! 86
Matthew 11:1–30

Week 39: The First Words That You Speak! 88
2 Timothy 2

Week 40: There's So Much We Don't Know! 92
Job 38

Week 41: A House Built for the Lord! 94
2 Chronicles 2 – 6

Week 42: Early Will I Seek Thee, My God!..........................96
Psalm 63

Week 43: Give Thanks to the Lord! 98
Psalm 136

Week 44: Have You Ever Been in the Lion's Den? 100
Daniel 6

Week 45: The Kingdom of Heaven Is at Hand!. .102
Matthew 3, 4

Week 46: How Will You Answer? 104
Matthew 27

Week 47: God Moments!. 106
Matthew 19

Week 48: Don't Give Up! Lift Jesus Up! Higher!. 108
John 12

Week 49: I Present to You My Sacrifice! 110
Romans 12

Week 50: The Story of Christmas Is Love! 112
Luke 2

Week 51: Lord Jesus, You Took My Blame! 114
John 1

Week 52: Near the End with Jesus Christ in Mind! 116
Hebrews 12, 13

Noteworthy Remembrances from the Lord 118
Thank you sincerely for taking this journey with me.. 119
A Little Bit about the Human Author 120

Enter thou into the joy of thy Lord!
—Matthew 25:21

Acknowledgments

I thank and acknowledge everyone who, in their own inimitable way, contributed to the writing of this devotional. I thank the pastors at Shekinah Revival Ministries whose weekly messages encouraged us to fulfill God's purpose in our lives. I thank past and present friends whose encouragement and prayer spurred me on to complete this offering to the Lord.

I offer thanks to Larry and Aleta, Herm and Nancy, Gene Key, Sister Agnes, Burt and Ella, David and Casandra, Tim, Roland and Carrie, Ruth and John, Doug and Linda, Matt and Esther, Bob and Linda, Kris, Tim and Rhoda, Matt and Carol, Fred and Sandy, past and present choir members, and countless others whose prayers have shown themselves to be indispensable in helping me "hear from the Lord." Special thanks go to my family for their prayers, encouragement, and patience during this writing. Thanks to Jack and Nancy, Henry and Leslie, Tim and Hilda, Jerry and Ena.

I want to especially thank the lady whom the Lord has given to me to be the joy of my life. I offer a very special acknowledgment of love and thankfulness to my wife, Joy, whose love and encouragement have allowed me to focus on and complete this labor of love. Thank you, Joy! I love you!

Introduction

I have found that it's the quiet moments with the Lord that produce in me the greatest epiphanies. It's not a loud earth-shattering announcement preceded by a heavenly blast of the trumpet, with a chorus of angels singing. Instead, when the Lord speaks directly to my spirit, it's a quiet, almost imperceptible nudging that increases my level of understanding about some nuance in my life. Sometimes, He is simply letting me know, on a spiritual level, that He is with me no matter where I may be at that moment. At such magnificent times, I am simply learning to say, "Speak Lord, for Your servant heareth" (1 Samuel 3:9).

In chapter 22 of the Book of Numbers, God reminds us that He used a donkey as a messenger to speak into the life of Balaam. In this book, may God use His scriptures, your personal, quiet moments of reflection, the words of the poems, and this messenger to speak deeply into your heart.

Remember, that this is *your* book of God Moments. Write down your musings, your visions, and your quiet feelings (Habakkuk 2:2). Allow your weekly writings to remind and encourage you to seek Him daily. When you seek Him, you *will* find Him, when you search for Him with all of your heart. (See Jeremiah 29:13.) During difficult moments of his life, King David encouraged himself in the Lord (1 Samuel 30:6). Please do likewise. During your quiet times, may you be encouraged as you re-read your own personal entries. May you remember with gladness God's blessings, His deliverances, and the beautiful impressions that He gently placed on your heart.

I pray and thank God in advance for the gentle intrusions that He will whisper to you during your times of consecration. As you spend time in God's Word, and as you read the weekly poems about the love and the greatness of our God, I pray that His very real presence will invade and saturate every fiber of your being! May you take the time to stop, to open the door of your heart, and to simply breathe Him in!

After you have spent time with the Lord and then enter a room, or begin your workday, or visit a doctor's office, or attend a picnic, may you sense the atmosphere change. May His light shine through you. May God allow you to be an encourager to those who don't yet know Him! May you be so filled with His essence, that His peace will overflow to those around you. May your example remind them that Jesus Christ is alive, that He is living in His saints in the person of the Holy Spirit, and that Christ Himself is seated on the right hand of God interceding on our behalf! Hallelujah! May those who know you be inspired to take the time to know Him more intimately.

Please remember, this little devotional is not about you, but it is for you. Year by year, week by week, and moment by moment, may you be drawn closer to our divine Creator. May you "Draw nigh to God" and allow Him to "draw nigh to you" (James 4:8).

May you find the time to simply be. Be still in the presence of your heavenly Father. Be assured that He is God (Psalm 46:10). Be comforted. Be at peace. As you spend time in God's Word and with the words of each poem, I pray that you will be willing and able to sit quietly at the conclusion of your readings and just listen to your Father's still, small voice (1 Kings 19:12). He is saying to you, in a myriad of ways, "Be aware; I love you so very much!" (John 3:16).

May you fully accept Jesus as the Son of God, the Christ, the Messiah, your Lord, and your Savior (1 John 5:12). May you know and believe that His blood has made you clean (Hebrews 9:14). May you accept His finished work on your behalf (John 19:30). May you know that Christ has done it all! Has paid it all! And may you know that He wants you to accept His free and perfect gift!

May the blessed person of the Holy Spirit guide you in your daily walk. Call on Him. He will answer. Embrace Him. He will reveal to you great and mighty things that you know not (Jeremiah 33:3). He will help you succeed. He wants you to "prosper and be in health, even as your soul prospers" (3 John 2)!

To receive God as your Father, Jesus as your Lord, and the Holy Spirit as your guide is a decision you make on your own. But you are not alone. Jesus has said, "I will never leave you or forsake you" (Hebrews 13:5). His presence is within you! His promises are holding you up! His power is keeping you alive! Remember, apart from Him, we can do nothing! Apart from Him, this little book would not exist. Apart from Him, we would be lost in our sin! Apart from Him, there would be no hope (John 15:5). But, praise God, we are filled with hope!

May your hope always be in God, our heavenly
Father, in Jesus Christ, the only begotten
Son of God, and in the blessed person of the
Holy Spirit. God is ready, willing, and able
to inhabit your heart, your mind, and your
soul the very moment you invite Him in!

Please invite Him in right now!
Today! This very moment!

Before the mountains were
brought forth, or ever Thou
hadst formed the earth and the
world, even from everlasting to
everlasting, Thou art God.

—Psalm 90:2

REASON 1—WEEK 1
In the Beginning with the End in Mind!
Reading for the Week: Genesis 1:1–31

A new year is upon us, a chance to start again.
A chance to say, "I love you!" to a dear and trusted friend!

A chance to set a brand-new goal according to God's will,
and see God's hand upon you as your new goal you fulfill!

You can choose this year to forgive someone
who you feel has done you wrong.
Then you'll lift up washed and holy hands and sing a brand-new song!

Do not take this year for granted, and don't focus on the past.
Embrace opportunities before you today; God's plans for you are vast!

Ask the Lord to open your eyes, and let you see what's truly real.
For reality is the Word of God! It's not based on how you feel!

Years ago, when God decided to make the heaven and earth,
He determined He'd give His Son for **you**; He
determined your value and worth!

New opportunities lie within you; and last year is far behind!
Begin this year by thanking your Lord! And keep the end in mind!

Your voice I long to hear ...
Impressions from the Lord, my God!

Sunday: _____

_____

_____

Monday: _____

_____

_____

Tuesday: _____

_____

_____

Wednesday: _____

_____

_____

Thursday: _____

_____

_____

Friday: _____

_____

_____

Saturday: _____

_____

_____

REASON 2—WEEK 2
Step Toward a Bright Tomorrow!
Reading for the Week: Deuteronomy 30:1–20

Your success is just a step away, and you must play your part!
There is something you're to do for God. Look deep within your heart!

The important work you've been assigned will take both time and skill!
When you take that step for the Lord your God, His purpose you'll fulfill!

It is not for "some others" to do it, for God chose you for this task!
To lead some out of bondage! "But why me?" I heard you ask.

There are some sad and special people whom only you can touch.
Long ago they had a heart for God, but someone hurt them so very much.

They still want to believe He's real, but they're filled with fear and sorrow.
They just can't see how bright can be their today or their tomorrow.

Their eyes right now are blinded by the enemy of their soul.
He wants them to deny God's truth. He wants to take control.

Your job is not to chase them, but to embrace them like a glove.
The Holy Spirit will show you how to lead them to God's love!

Your voice I long to hear ...
Impressions from the Lord, my God!

Sunday: _____
_____
_____

Monday: _____
_____
_____

Tuesday: _____
_____
_____

Wednesday: _____
_____
_____

Thursday: _____
_____
_____

Friday: _____
_____
_____

Saturday: _____
_____
_____

REASON 3—WEEK 3
You Will Never Walk Alone!
Reading for the Week: Joshua 1:1–18

As you pursue God's plans for you, you're
bombarded with doubts and worry!
You want hard evidence of His pure love, and you need it in a hurry!

Did you really hear Him in your spirit? Did
you hear God's still small voice?
Did He really say you are to lead His charge?
Are you really God's perfect choice?

Are you sure that God is still with you? Are you sure you will not fail?
Can you stand firm in your courage when
you feel so defeated and so frail?

Can you really stand strong and victorious
when you feel so tired and weak?
When you heard Him say He'd be with you, are
you sure it was God you heard speak?

Stop right now! (Pause) Believe that God is inside
of you, even though you are but dust.
Believe that God's ways are perfect! You Know His ways are just!

The battle lines are settled. Don't lose heart; don't be afraid.
Our God was not mistaken when He chose you to lead His brigade.

So, in this third week of the brand-new year,
when you can't face life on your own,
Rejoice, for Jesus Christ walks with you; and you'll never walk alone!

Your voice I long to hear ...
Impressions from the Lord, my God!

Sunday: _____
_____
_____

Monday: _____
_____
_____

Tuesday: _____
_____
_____

Wednesday: _____
_____
_____

Thursday: _____
_____
_____

Friday: _____
_____
_____

Saturday: _____
_____
_____

REASON 4—WEEK 4
You Made It Through the Battle!
Reading for the Week: Judges 15, 16

Though a thousand came against him, with a jawbone he prevailed.
Samson was victorious, and God's enemies were assailed!

Now you want to be an example: to spread the Gospel News!
You feel, since you put on the whole armor of
God, there's no way that you can lose.

Take care, my friend and listen to words I feel compelled to say.
You made it through one battle; the next war is not far away!

The enemy will use people; he'll use lies, guilt, and shame,
to come against the saints of God, and smear each righteous name.

You know all the schemes he uses, so don't fall into his snare.
Your Lord gave you the mind of Christ! He's already made you aware!

Believe that God stands with you! Know He'll lead you safely through.
You'll receive eternal victory when you've done as God says "Do!"

You will make it through each battle with your adversary in retreat.
For the Lord is fighting for you, and He will never face defeat!

Your voice I long to hear ...
Impressions from the Lord, my God!

Sunday: _____

_____

_____

Monday: _____

_____

_____

Tuesday: _____

_____

_____

Wednesday: _____

_____

_____

Thursday: _____

_____

_____

Friday: _____

_____

_____

Saturday: _____

_____

_____

REASON 5—WEEK 5
God's Love is in the Making!
Reading for the Week: Ruth 1, 2, 3, 4

From time to time you've wondered which direction to pursue;
is your mission field in America? In Africa, Asia, or Peru?

Will you spend your life in solitude? Will God provide a mate?
Since God really knows all answers, should you ask Him, "What's your fate?"

You've decided to follow the will of God. Meet Him each day in prayer.
Like Ruth, place all your trust in Him every day and everywhere.

God's love is always working; He alone makes life complete!
Simply trust Him to prepare for you a life that's full, and pure, and sweet!

When God's Spirit tells you something, trust His Word and never cease.
For with Christ as Lord and Savior, you'll experience His blessed peace!

There may be times when you'll feel lonely; there
may be times when you'll feel sad.
But with Jesus as your ever-present Friend,
His presence will make you glad!

God's love is in the making. He's pouring love on you right now!
Just believe Him and receive Him; Christ will lead you through somehow!

Your voice I long to hear ...
Impressions from the Lord, my God!

Sunday: _____
_____
_____

Monday: _____
_____
_____

Tuesday: _____
_____
_____

Wednesday: _____
_____
_____

Thursday: _____
_____
_____

Friday: _____
_____
_____

Saturday: _____
_____
_____

REASON 6—WEEK 6
Faith Is Trusting God During Trials!
Reading for the Week: Job 1, 2, 3

Have you read about God's servant Job? He
was both trustworthy and devout!
Did you know the enemy tried to steal his joy and totally wipe Job out?

Did you know that during those rugged
trials, Job's faith refused to waver?
He trusted in the God of love and received the Father's favor.

So when, not if, the trials come, reject both fear and dread.
Your heavenly Father loves you and knows every hair upon your head.

He won't allow temptation to ensnare those who belong to Him.
His nail-pierced feet will lead you through paths that may seem dim.

Our God sees past the darkness; have faith, He'll lead you through.
Rest in His awesome power; your God is watching over you!

Best friends just cannot understand; they'll
think you've done some wrong.
But when God turns your world around,
He'll leave you standing strong.

God sees what's on the horizon; He knows what's around each bend.
Trust God through every trial. He'll lead you safely to life's end!

Your voice I long to hear ...
Impressions from the Lord, my God!

Sunday: _____
_____
_____

Monday: _____
_____
_____

Tuesday: _____
_____
_____

Wednesday: _____
_____
_____

Thursday: _____
_____
_____

Friday: _____
_____
_____

Saturday: _____
_____
_____

REASON 7—WEEK 7
Faith Is Trusting God All the Time!
Reading for the Week: Job 42

Have you read about God's servant Job? He
was tempted beyond all measure!
He would not curse the Lord his God, since
praising God was his true pleasure!

Though it seemed to most that Job had lost
his family, friends, and wealth,
in the end, God doubled all His gifts to Job,
and restored Job's failing health.

For God is our Provider; He supplies our every need.
He knows before we ask Him. He's a faithful Friend indeed!

Do not allow uncertainty to fill your mind with fear.
Trust the Lord with all your heart; your Father's always near!

If you start to feel some doubt about God's merciful grace,
remember God gave up His Son; His sacrifice in your place!

Pray for those who cannot see God's gift to every nation.
Declare, in faith, that it's God's own hand protecting His very creation!

Faith is trusting the God of all time, for He sees eternally!
And He's prepared a heavenly home for you,
where you'll spend eternity!

Your voice I long to hear ...
Impressions from the Lord, my God!

Sunday: _____

_____

_____

Monday: _____

_____

_____

Tuesday: _____

_____

_____

Wednesday: _____

_____

_____

Thursday: _____

_____

_____

Friday: _____

_____

_____

Saturday: _____

_____

_____

Reason 8—Week 8
Sing a Song to the Lord, Your God!
Reading for the Week: Psalm 27

Wake up in the morning with a song upon your heart.
Remember, there's no better way for your new day to start.

For even the birds sing praises at the rising of the sun.
Give the Lord all of your worship! Praise Him for all He's done!

Sing to the Lord a new song. Sing from the depths of your soul.
For it's His grace that saved you; God's love has made you whole.

Don't let the rocks out-praise you; give thanks with each new breath.
For He alone has given you the keys to life over death.

Sing a song to the Lord, your God. He's worthy of adoration.
Lift up your voice in gratitude, in love, and joyful declaration!

The Lord is your light and your salvation, your shield from every fear!
The Lord is the strength of your life. Rejoice! He's ever near!

So, sing a song to the Lord, your God, King Jesus; God alone!
He will gladly receive you as His precious child
as you bow before His throne!

Your voice I long to hear ...
Impressions from the Lord, my God!

Sunday: _____
_____
_____

Monday: _____
_____
_____

Tuesday: _____
_____
_____

Wednesday: _____
_____
_____

Thursday: _____
_____
_____

Friday: _____
_____
_____

Saturday: _____
_____
_____

REASON 9—WEEK 9
Look at God's Beauty All Around You!
Reading for the Week: Psalm 19

Look at God's beauty all around you. His
existence just can't be ignored!
For no one can do all the things that God does.
No one else is our Savior and Lord!

The heavens sing God's praises! The mighty oceans roar His name!
Of everything that's ever been, there are not
two that are identically the same.

Even twins are not identical. Just speak with them and see.
The differences in each one proclaim God's limitless creativity.

Roses have their beauty; sunsets, sunrises, too!
Each one of them is different. Each one shows something new.

There is a sweet uniqueness in everything God has made.
Each somehow includes a facet of God's awesome beauty on parade!

The heavens sing God's praises! The oceans roar His power!
Look for the Lord in you and me, and in every bird and flower.

Just look at all there is to see, God's awesomeness and might!
Praise God with words coming from your mouth.
May they be acceptable in His sight!

Your voice I long to hear ...
Impressions from the Lord, my God!

Sunday: _____

_____

_____

Monday: _____

_____

_____

Tuesday: _____

_____

_____

Wednesday: _____

_____

_____

Thursday: _____

_____

_____

Friday: _____

_____

_____

Saturday: _____

_____

_____

Reason 10—Week 10
Whose Plans Will You Follow This week?
Reading for the Week: Jeremiah 29

Whose plans will you follow this week; before
whom, my friend, will you bow?
Whom do you know who's all-powerful? Who
alone knows what's coming now?

Thank God for each new morning; thank Him for last night's rest!
Thank God, He didn't grant you the plans that you thought were best!

God knows the plans He has for you; He'll
help you prosper and succeed.
But you must willingly recognize that it's
His power that you sorely need.

So, before you grab your planner, listen quietly for His plan.
Then write down all of His words to you, in ways you'll understand.

Perform each task, one at a time, until you have completed
the plan God has for you today; then let your heart be seated.

Don't fret about the next task that God might have for you!
He'll give you strength and time and skill before the task is due.

So call upon the Lord your God. Seek Him; He will be found!
He will lovingly care for you, as He turns your world around!

Whose plans will you follow this week; before
whom, my friend, will you bow?
Who else do you know who's all-loving? Receive
your Father's intense love for you, right now!

Your voice I long to hear ...
Impressions from the Lord, my God!

Sunday: _____
_____
_____

Monday: _____
_____
_____

Tuesday: _____
_____
_____

Wednesday: _____
_____
_____

Thursday: _____
_____
_____

Friday: _____
_____
_____

Saturday: _____
_____
_____

REASON 11—WEEK 11
Lord Jesus, Awaken Us from Sleep!
Reading for the Week: John 11

Lord Jesus, awaken us from our sleep. Help us to see what is true.
And lead us not to paths of death, but life, by closely following You.

In John 11:11, You spoke to us of sleep.
And You went to wake up Lazarus, from the pit of death so deep.

For Lazarus was a friend of Yours, whose sickness made him die.
When You came and restored his life, You
brought praise to our God Most High.

When we get sick and tired of things not going as we would hope,
remind us of Your power that You give to help us cope.

During times when we are unaware, during times when we are asleep,
Lord Jesus, come and wake us up; and remind us of Your love so deep.

We know You always see us, and You hear our faintest prayers.
We ask You, Lord, to awaken us from doubts,
and fears, and worries, and cares.

Lord Jesus, awaken us from sleep; make our hearts alive again!
We'll gladly give God all the glory! As did Lazarus, Your friend!

Your voice I long to hear ...
Impressions from the Lord, my God!

Sunday: _____

_____

Monday: _____

_____

Tuesday: _____

_____

Wednesday: _____

_____

Thursday: _____

_____

Friday: _____

_____

_____

Saturday: _____

_____

_____

REASON 12—WEEK 12
What Do You Have to Show for Your "Show and Tell" to God?
Reading for the Week: Luke 19

This year is now just twelve weeks old, and what do you have to show?
Did you use the blessings you received? Did
you help to make them grow?

Did you choose to bury your talents in a napkin in the ground?
So you could go and dig them up when the Master came to town?

Did you use the talents you received for personal wealth or fame?
Or were they used to serve your God and bless His holy name?

Deep inside, you know the answer. It will come as no surprise.
The King of kings and Lord of lords knows it all; for He is wise!

Since Jesus Christ has blessed you with those skills that you possess,
you're to give Him what belongs to Him; you dare not offer less!

Watch and see what God will do, if you'll proclaim your trust…
in the only One in all the world who's loving, kind, faithful, and just!

Decide to be God's faithful servant. Choose to make His glory known.
Then you'll have lots to show and tell as you stand before His throne!

Your voice I long to hear ...
Impressions from the Lord, my God!

Sunday: _____

_____

_____

Monday: _____

_____

_____

Tuesday: _____

_____

_____

Wednesday: _____

_____

_____

Thursday: _____

_____

_____

Friday: _____

_____

_____

Saturday: _____

_____

_____

REASON 13—WEEK 13
We Serve as God's Ambassadors!
Reading for the Week: Romans 8:1–39

There is no condemnation for those in Jesus Christ
who walk in thankfulness to God, for His perfect sacrifice!

We're blessed to live in constant fellowship with our Redeemer King!
Christ bore our sins, and He paid our debts; Himself, God's offering!

We've been adopted by the Father! We're
joint heirs with God's own Son!
We've been justified and glorified; eternal victory's been won!

We're to serve as God's ambassadors. We're to serve to reveal His light!
We're to serve to help His followers learn how to choose what's right.

Our task this week is simple. It's to be esteemed and highly adored.
We're to serve as guides along the path to Jesus Christ, our Lord!

The way, we know, is narrow, but all may enter in,
when we follow after Jesus and choose not to follow sin.

So, serve as God's ambassador; declare His awesome beauty!
Lead His saints to gates of glory and fulfill your heavenly duty!

Your voice I long to hear ...
Impressions from the Lord, my God!

Sunday: _____
_____
_____

Monday: _____
_____
_____

Tuesday: _____
_____
_____

Wednesday: _____
_____
_____

Thursday: _____
_____
_____

Friday: _____
_____
_____

Saturday: _____
_____
_____

God Moments

Acquire more intimate knowledge of
God's totally awesome presence ...

Spend some quiet time with Him ...

Learn to hear His voice ...

REASON 14—WEEK 14
Remember, We Are Victorious in God!
Reading for the Week: 2 Chronicles 19, 20

Remember, we are victorious, for we chose the winning side!
We chose to follow God's dear Son as our Savior and our Guide!

Last week is a fading memory, and we're glad we made it through.
But let's not rest on past successes. There is a
lot more work for each of us to do!

God's assignment for us is not a burden. The task
we've chosen is definitely not a chore.
Remember, it's our freewill offering to willingly
fight for the One whom we adore!

So, trust Father God to sustain you, though
the work's not always easy or fun.
For the battle is the Lord's, our God's, and He's already won!

Your Father goes before you, and He protects you from behind.
You're to trust in the Lord with all your heart
and with all your soul and mind.

You're to sing loud your hallelujahs, and shout boldly with songs of praise!
And serve with valor, your King of kings, the Great Ancient of Days!

Remember, you are victorious! Remember, you are God's child!
He loves to lavish His love on you, for through
Christ's blood, you're now reconciled!

Your voice I long to hear ...
Impressions from the Lord, my God!

Sunday: _____

_____

_____

Monday: _____

_____

_____

Tuesday: _____

_____

_____

Wednesday: _____

_____

_____

Thursday: _____

_____

_____

Friday: _____

_____

_____

Saturday: _____

_____

_____

REASON 15—WEEK 15
Leave Your Troubles in Gethsemane!
Reading for the Week: Matthew 26

Leave your troubles in Gethsemane, on the rock where Jesus prayed.
Trust the Lord to pull you through; you must not feel dismayed.

The next time you are troubled, know that Christ faced troubles too,
and He left them in the garden, and His Father pulled Him through.

Remember that Christ has promised He would not leave you alone.
And, He sent His Holy Spirit to be your very own.

Just listen to the counsel of Him Who knows all things,
for your Counselor knows far in advance just what your future brings.

If you pray and ask the Father which roads He'd have you take,
which streets and highways to avoid, then you'll make no mistake.

The times we tend to err are those times we think we know.
And thus we fail to ask our Father about the way He'd have us go!

So come to God in humbleness, with all your sins laid bare.
Leave your troubles in Gethsemane, and receive your Father's care!

Your voice I long to hear ...
Impressions from the Lord, my God!

Sunday: _____
_____
_____

Monday: _____
_____
_____

Tuesday: _____
_____
_____

Wednesday: _____
_____
_____

Thursday: _____
_____
_____

Friday: _____
_____
_____

Saturday: _____
_____
_____

REASON 16—WEEK 16
Complete This Week's Task!
Reading for the Week: Exodus 17

This is the week for you to seek God's next appointed task.
And if the work seems much too large, it depends on whom you ask.

For in the mighty hands of God, every huge job becomes small.
For God created all that is, and He is your All in all.

Raise up your hands, see God work; just watch what He will do!
Ask friends, in prayer, to hold you up. Let them help you make it through!

Determine that you will complete the task with God's supernatural aid.
For God breeds nothing but success in every creature He has made.

In six days God created the world and then took time to rest.
So when you rest upon His strength, you'll do His very best.

God's best is so much greater than you or I could ever dream.
Trust Him fully in this week's task to accomplish the extreme.

And when your task is over, look back on what He's done.
And give thanks to God the Father, and to Jesus Christ, His Son.

Your voice I long to hear …
Impressions from the Lord, my God!

Sunday: _____

_____

_____

Monday: _____

_____

_____

Tuesday: _____

_____

_____

Wednesday: _____

_____

_____

Thursday: _____

_____

_____

Friday: _____

_____

_____

Saturday: _____

_____

_____

REASON 17—WEEK 17
Come Holy Spirit!
Reading for the Week: John 14

Come Holy Spirit! Fill each and every corner of my being.
Guide me and direct me. Help me see as You are seeing!

Help me to see the hungry, and the thirsty, and the lost.
Help me choose to follow You, no matter what the cost!

Blessed Holy Spirit, come and speak with me today,
and declare the Father's task for me, and direct me in His way!

For my Father has a task for me, perfect in its design.
He wants me to follow willingly His plan that's so divine.

Help me really know You. Implant Your peace within my heart.
Help me grasp the Gospel message. Help me share how great Thou art!

Help me worship at God's altar. Help me bow before His throne.
May I listen to God's still small voice. May I trust in Him alone.

Welcome, Holy Spirit! It's Your guiding presence I want most!
Abide in me forever, Comforter and Holy Ghost!

Your voice I long to hear ...
Impressions from the Lord, my God!

Sunday: _____
_____
_____

Monday: _____
_____
_____

Tuesday: _____
_____
_____

Wednesday: _____
_____
_____

Thursday: _____
_____
_____

Friday: _____
_____
_____

Saturday: _____
_____
_____

REASON 18—WEEK 18
Jesus! Jesus! Lord Jesus!
Reading for the Week: Mark 15, 16

Jesus, Jesus, Lord Jesus! For me You suffered, bled, and died.
For every sin of the entire world, You, Lord, were crucified.

You are our Blessed Redeemer; You're God's only begotten Son,
sent down to earth from heaven as God's purely righteous One.

You're the King who came to save us. And,
Your blood has washed us clean.
Your only earthly ambition was for Your Heavenly Father to be seen.

Your Father named You Jesus, our Messiah and our King,
our Emmanuel and Savior, our Christ, our everything!

You are patient, kind, and humble, and some might think it kind of odd,
That not a priest, but a centurion said, "Truly
this man was the Son of God."

When You descended into Sheol, You took
back the keys of life and death.
Oh, Jesus, precious Jesus, we worship You with each new breath.

You then ascended into heaven when Your work here was complete!
And took Your rightful place, my King, upon God's judgment seat.

Your voice I long to hear ...
Impressions from the Lord, my God!

Sunday: _____
_____
_____

Monday: _____
_____
_____

Tuesday: _____
_____
_____

Wednesday: _____
_____
_____

Thursday: _____
_____
_____

Friday: _____
_____
_____

Saturday: _____
_____
_____

REASON 19—WEEK 19
Blessed Are You!
Reading for the Week: Matthew 5

Blessed are the peacemakers, and blessed are the meek.
They shall be called the children of God, for it's the Father's face they seek.

Blessed is the man who trusts the Lord, and not upon himself;
who places the will of God foremost, his own will upon the shelf.

Blessed is the woman who trusts the Lord, and not upon her beauty,
who strives to be a woman of God, a divinely appointed duty.

Blessed is the boy who trusts the Lord, and not upon his skill;
who serves the Lord with all his heart and seeks the Father's will.

Blessed is the girl who trusts the Lord and not upon her mind,
who knows that God alone bestows the wisdom for all mankind.

Blessed is the saint who trusts the Lord, and not upon society's praise,
who works to please Almighty God and serves Him all his days.

Blessed are you who trust the Lord, who depend upon His blessing.
For you'll receive God's bounty, His presence, His caressing.

Your voice I long to hear ...
Impressions from the Lord, my God!

Sunday: _____

_____

_____

Monday: _____

_____

_____

Tuesday: _____

_____

_____

Wednesday: _____

_____

_____

Thursday: _____

_____

_____

Friday: _____

_____

_____

Saturday: _____

_____

_____

REASON 20—WEEK 20
Expectations!
Reading for the Week: Luke 1

Expect to witness miracles over the next upcoming days.
Expect that you will find the Lord when you bow in humble praise.

Expect that you will see Him when He is least expected,
for He wants to be found of you, so you will never feel neglected.

Expect Him in the morning or in the middle of the night,
for God does love His time with you, and you are His delight.

Expect that God will bless you, in ways you may not see,
through those who love you dearly as they pray on bended knee.

Expect that God surrounds you with His love so kind and true,
that no harm will befall you; your Father's watching out for you!

Expect the unexpected, for God's ways can't be explained.
He's Awesome and beyond our words; our God can't be restrained!

Expect to walk with Jesus. He's your Lord, Savior, and Guide.
Expect He'll always love you; you're His beloved and faithful bride!

Your voice I long to hear ...
Impressions from the Lord, my God!

Sunday: _____
_____
_____

Monday: _____
_____
_____

Tuesday: _____
_____
_____

Wednesday: _____
_____
_____

Thursday: _____
_____
_____

Friday: _____
_____
_____

Saturday: _____
_____
_____

Reason 21—Week 21
But Why, Lord?
Reading for the Week: Isaiah 55

"But why, Lord?" is a question that's forever plagued humankind.
We seem to think we have some right to know what's on God's mind!

We forgot that we have not created Him, but God created us.
And yet we think we have some right to complain and raise a fuss.

We know our God is merciful. That He alone is wise and good.
Still, we gripe when things don't happen in
the way we think they should.

Our eyes can't see this fallen world through His most perfect view.
So help us, Lord, to trust You more and to see things as You do.

As heaven is higher than the earth, Your thoughts are higher than ours.
Your words will accomplish all that You please,
through Your supernatural powers!

We're to seek You while You may be found;
we're to call while You are near.
Though we can't understand Your mysterious ways,
trust in You helps remove the fear.

So when we say, "But why, Lord?" help us start to recognize
That Your ways are not our ways.
You created the sun, the moon, the universe, the skies!

Your voice I long to hear ...
Impressions from the Lord, my God!

Sunday: _____

_____

_____

Monday: _____

_____

_____

Tuesday: _____

_____

_____

Wednesday: _____

_____

_____

Thursday: _____

_____

_____

Friday: _____

_____

_____

Saturday: _____

_____

_____

REASON 22—WEEK 22
Let the Peace of the Lord Fill Your Mind!
Reading for the Week: Psalm 133, 134

May you take the time this week to sit and be at peace.
For in the thing that we call life, the pressures never cease.

Let the peace of God just fill you up; rest in God's security.
Bless the Lord! Praise His name! In Christ, your soul's found liberty!

May you strive to not be anxious; choose not to live in strife.
You can choose to follow Jesus! Allow Him to forever change your life.

His Words are filled with power; His Words will make you new.
His Words will help you shout out loud, "Lord,
we're glad we belong to You!"

Let not your heart be troubled; neither let it be afraid.
Receive with Christ's authority a peace that will not fade.

Rest for a while and listen. Let God's peace fill up your mind.
Receive the gift of your Father's love. Leave
the turmoil of this world far behind!

Behold how good and pleasant it is to sit with One so kind!
And allow the blessed peace of God to overflow your heart and mind!

Your voice I long to hear ...
Impressions from the Lord, my God!

Sunday: _____

_____

_____

Monday: _____

_____

_____

Tuesday: _____

_____

_____

Wednesday: _____

_____

_____

Thursday: _____

_____

_____

Friday: _____

_____

_____

Saturday: _____

_____

_____

REASON 23—WEEK 23
You're Perfect in His Sight!
Reading for the Week: 2 Corinthians 5

This week the Lord wants you to know you're perfect in His sight.
For He has made you guiltless; He's bathed you in purest light.

You are an earthly tabernacle, in whom God's grace abounds.
His eternal house, not made with hands, whom the Spirit of God surrounds.

Whether man or woman, boy or girl, you fit His mold completely.
For when God formed you in the womb, He fashioned you discretely.

The world may seek to find some flaw in your smile, your walk, or your face.
In God's eyes, you're incredibly stunning! Everything is in perfect place!

Your eyes, your hair, your mind, your teeth, your emotions, and your skin,
are all as God designed them; your exquisite beauty lies within.

He's called you His ambassador; you walk by faith, not sight.
You are His new creation. You're clothed in purest white.

The world may not appreciate your attributes, heaven sent.
But when God called you His lovely bride, that's exactly what He meant!

Your voice I long to hear ...
Impressions from the Lord, my God!

Sunday: _____

_____

_____

Monday: _____

_____

_____

Tuesday: _____

_____

_____

Wednesday: _____

_____

_____

Thursday: _____

_____

_____

Friday: _____

_____

_____

Saturday: _____

_____

_____

REASON 24—WEEK 24
This Week!
Reading for the Week: Luke 9

This week may have its troubles; you won't know where to turn.
But fix your eyes on Jesus; He has lots for you to learn.

God wants to spend time with you; He has knowledge to impart.
So, as He speaks so tenderly, listen closely to His heart.

Spend the whole day with Jesus. Let Him infiltrate your soul.
Dwell with Him, and He in you. Let that be your only goal.

He knows the plans He has for you, each step along life's way!
And when you trust and follow Him, you won't be led astray.

Take time to sit with Jesus … No agenda … No request …
Sit patiently before Him and receive His very best.

Be still and know the "Beloved Son", whom the Father's voice declared,
and one day you will join Him in that place that He's prepared.

For Jesus is your Master; He's the Truth, the Life, the Way!
He only wants what's best for you, so cling to Him each day.

This week may have its troubles, but you know just where to turn.
Fix your eyes and mind on Jesus; He has lots for you to learn.

Your voice I long to hear ...
Impressions from the Lord, my God!

Sunday: _____

_____

_____

Monday: _____

_____

_____

Tuesday: _____

_____

_____

Wednesday: _____

_____

_____

Thursday: _____

_____

_____

Friday: _____

_____

_____

Saturday: _____

_____

_____

REASON 25—WEEK 25
The Seasons Are a – Turning!
Reading for the Week: Isaiah 60

The seasons are a - turning, and, yes, it's plain to see
that the Spirit of God is moving over all humanity.

There are changes on the horizon; you can feel them in the air
if we take the time to listen, when we take the time in prayer.

The seasons are passing swiftly, and a new one's just begun.
May we choose to be made more aware of God our Father and His Son.

Arise, shine, for His light has come, and His glory is being revealed
on the faces of the righteous, for by His precious blood they are sealed!

God's people shall all be righteous, and they shall inherit the land.
They are the work of God's planting. They are the work of His hand.

The clock is quickly ticking; don't let this season pass you by.
Listen for your Master's calling! Respond to your Master's cry!

The seasons are a - turning, and there is no time to waste.
Come quickly to embrace your Lord; now is a time for haste.

Your voice I long to hear ...
Impressions from the Lord, my God!

Sunday: _____

_____

_____

Monday: _____

_____

_____

Tuesday: _____

_____

_____

Wednesday: _____

_____

_____

Thursday: _____

_____

_____

Friday: _____

_____

_____

_____

Saturday: _____

_____

_____

Reason 26—Week 26
Lord, May I Never Become So Proud!
Reading for the Week: Proverbs 16

Lord, may I never become so proud of gifts You've given to me,
that I allow myself to be blinded to needs You'd have me see.

For everyone who is proud in heart is an abomination.
But those who fear and please You, Lord, receive divine salvation.

Bless me to be humble, Lord, with a heart that's teachable.
Grace me to be loving, Lord, with a heart that's reachable.

Let me never be arrogant, Lord, or seek to please the crowd.
May I live to give You glory for the blessings You've allowed.

Alert me, Heavenly Father, the very moment I start to drift.
Redirect my heart to honor You while displaying Your generous gift.

Pride goes before destruction; a haughty spirit before a fall.
Give me ears to hear, my God, and to heed Your faintest call.

And if I fail to see or feel the gentle nudging of Your Spirit,
please come inside and whisper, Lord, so that my soul may hear it.

And may I never be filled with pride, but teach me to be wise.
May I follow You as Master and Lord, 'til You bid me to arise!

Your voice I long to hear ...
Impressions from the Lord, my God!

Sunday: _____
_____
_____

Monday: _____
_____
_____

Tuesday: _____
_____
_____

Wednesday: _____
_____
_____

Thursday: _____
_____
_____

Friday: _____
_____
_____

Saturday: _____
_____
_____

God Moments

The heavens declare God's glory! Humbly increase your appreciation of His indescribable beauty and power. Just be ...

Reason 27—Week 27
We Praise You Because You're Good!
Reading for the Week: Matthew 19, 20

We praise You because You're good, Lord God;
we praise You because You're good!
The many great things that You've done for
us are simply misunderstood.

And yet You love us as we are! We are a pitiable lot!
For when we should be thanking You, thanking You, Lord, we're not!

We find so much to gripe about, like people who have no hope.
We murmur, complain; we moan and groan like we've lost our will to cope.

We're like ancient children of Israel who doubted again and again.
Who didn't know if You would deliver them.
Who'd forgotten how good You had been.

Let us be as the determined blind men who
begged to receive their sight.
For they knew that You were gracious and
good, and filled with heavenly might!

We all need to know You, Jesus. To recall the price that You paid.
For all our sins, for all of time, upon You, our Lord, were laid.

We take time this week to thank You for mistreatment You withstood.
We praise You because You're good, Lord God.
We praise You because You're good!

Your voice I long to hear ...
Impressions from the Lord, my God!

Sunday: _____

_____

_____

Monday: _____

_____

_____

Tuesday: _____

_____

_____

Wednesday: _____

_____

_____

Thursday: _____

_____

_____

Friday: _____

_____

_____

Saturday: _____

_____

_____

REASON 28—WEEK 28
I Didn't Know—But You Did!
Reading for the Week: Judges 4, 5

I did not know if I would make it, but You led me through last week.
You never, ever failed me, though at times my way looked bleak.

You helped me focus upon Your Son, and not on trials that came.
You assured me of my victory through the name above all names.

While Barak relied on Deborah, Deborah relied on You
to defeat the enemies of the living God, as only our God could do!

I too can't make it without You, Lord. I don't even want to try.
I choose to follow You, dear God, and never question why.

You know just where I'm going, before each day begins.
You know if there'll be losses; You know if there'll be wins.

May I keep my eyes on Jesus Christ as He leads me day by day.
He is the Life. He is the Truth. He's the lamp that lights my way!

I do not know, but You do, Lord, just how each week will go.
But lovingly and daily You lead me. Father God I love You so!

Your voice I long to hear ...
Impressions from the Lord, my God!

Sunday: _____

_____

_____

Monday: _____

_____

_____

Tuesday: _____

_____

_____

Wednesday: _____

_____

_____

Thursday: _____

_____

_____

Friday: _____

_____

_____

Saturday: _____

_____

_____

REASON 29—WEEK 29
Come Out and Just Be You!
Reading for the Week: Esther 2

Come out and just be you, my friend, for whom else should you be?
Reveal that you are a child of God. You're a child of royalty!

You're a child of God Almighty, born on your special date.
You were not born too early, and you were not born too late!

He'll unveil you when He's ready, and all the world will know
it was God who purified you; He, Who vanquished every foe!

God's timing, it was perfect, part of His grand master scheme.
You're here for such a time as this, a vital part of His great dream.

So be whom God has made you. He's your Father, you're the child of the King!
And through the blood of Jesus, your whole life is a beautiful thing!

You have no other master. You're unchained; you've been set free.
Because your Father loves you, you'll reign with Him for eternity!

So worship your heavenly Father! Praise Him openly! Remove all doubt!
And be who God made you to be. Let His presence, in you, come out!

Your voice I long to hear ...
Impressions from the Lord, my God!

Sunday: _____

_____

_____

Monday: _____

_____

_____

Tuesday: _____

_____

_____

Wednesday: _____

_____

_____

Thursday: _____

_____

_____

Friday: _____

_____

_____

Saturday: _____

_____

_____

REASON 30—WEEK 30
My Meat Is to Do Thy Will, Lord God!
John 4

My meat is to do Thy will, Lord God, to boldly finish my course.
Stride by stride, You are my guide; You are my only source.

My prize is near, and soon I'll hear those beautiful words, "Well done!"
With heavenly force, I'll finish the course that You led me to run!

There are things I am to do, oh God; I must first take time to hear
of places and faces You'd have me touch, as You make my paths clear.

When I must go through Samaria, or to prisons, or to Rome,
may Your peace abide within me, 'til You bring me safely home!

May I hear Your still, small voice, my King, set goals for me today!
And as I take each precious step, I'll know it's You Who led the way!

If I'll delight myself in You, You'll grant the desires of my heart!
My earnest desire is to please You, Lord; to faithfully do my part.

My meat is to do Thy will, Lord God, to let my light shine bright.
Then others will be drawn to You, to behold Your power and might!

Your voice I long to hear ...
Impressions from the Lord, my God!

Sunday: _____
_____
_____

Monday: _____
_____
_____

Tuesday: _____
_____
_____

Wednesday: _____
_____
_____

Thursday: _____
_____
_____

Friday: _____
_____
_____

Saturday: _____
_____
_____

REASON 31—WEEK 31
Your Next Assignment, "Go!"
Matthew 28:16–20

There are hurting people around you who need a friendly smile.
They need to know that someone cares for just a little while.

Their life has not been easy; they "grin and bear it", as they say.
They believe Christ is their Savior, and they pray to God each day!

Not looking for a handout, they just need to be acknowledged.
They're not striving to impress us with some skills they learned in college.

They're looking for true friendship, a task that seems so strenuous!
And all too often what they see are smiles so disingenuous.

So, if you have a moment, and if you would like to do some good,
then be their friend and dig right in, just as our Savior would!

Your next assignment may be to go and reach some unreached nation
and to show someone the love of Christ on your very next vacation!

Go tell them that God loves them. Go tell them He is real!
And remind them He's alive and well, in spite of what they hear or feel!

Your voice I long to hear ...
Impressions from the Lord, my God!

Sunday: _____

_____

_____

Monday: _____

_____

_____

Tuesday: _____

_____

_____

Wednesday: _____

_____

_____

Thursday: _____

_____

_____

_____

Friday: _____

_____

_____

Saturday: _____

_____

_____

REASON 32—WEEK 32
God's Gift for Today!
Galatians 5:1–26

Did you receive a gift today; A gift made just for you?
It is a present from our heavenly Father, Who devised the way to make you new.

His gift was wrapped in swaddling clothes; it had no bows or string.
But He's the greatest present that our God could ever bring!

He is God's gift of love and grace, and mercy's in Him too!
And joy and peace and gentleness, and still God wasn't through.

He is the gift of patience and of goodness beyond measure.
God also gave the gift of faith, just because it was His pleasure!

Next, He added meekness, so we'd have no cause to boast!
And then the gift of temperance, and the mind of the Holy Ghost!

Did you receive God's gift today? Make sure you don't abuse it!
It's a present from our Almighty God! He's shown us how to use it!

The world may say, "It's nothing! It's just some fantasy in your head!"
But the gift, you know, is God's own Son. The One Who rose up from the dead!

Your voice I long to hear ...
Impressions from the Lord, my God!

Sunday: _____

_____

_____

Monday: _____

_____

_____

Tuesday: _____

_____

_____

Wednesday: _____

_____

_____

Thursday: _____

_____

_____

Friday: _____

_____

_____

Saturday: _____

_____

_____

REASON 33—WEEK 33
Hallelujah! It's Time to Ascend!
1 Thessalonians 4, 5

Did you hear today's weather forecast, about the marvelous, upcoming sight?
About the Lord's return from heaven in His robe so pure and white?

How there will be a noise from heaven? It will sound just like a shout.
How the dead in Christ will rise to the sky,
and their graves will be emptied out?

How the voice of the Archangel and a trumpet's mighty blast
will let all those who wait for Him know it's time for the Lord's return - at last!

All saints of God who serve the Lord, they will not feel despair,
for they will be the next to rise, and to meet Christ in the air!

God loves us, for we chose His Son as atonement for our sin.
Because of the blood of Jesus Christ, we win, my friend, we win!

Hallelujah, it's almost time to ascend, and to abide in our heavenly place,
where we'll worship the Lord without ceasing, and gladly bow before His face!

So rejoice, ye saints, for evermore, and in everything give thanks!
Our Lord's returning in the clouds, with His mighty angels at His flanks!

Your voice I long to hear ...
Impressions from the Lord, my God!

Sunday: _____
_____
_____

Monday: _____
_____
_____

Tuesday: _____
_____
_____

Wednesday: _____
_____
_____

Thursday: _____
_____
_____

Friday: _____
_____
_____

Saturday: _____
_____
_____

REASON 34—WEEK 34
Learning How to Trust!
Romans 8:26–39

There are times when it is so hard to trust, when even our best friends fail us.
May we turn to Jesus, the living Christ, as trials and woes assail us.

We conquer through Him Who loves us; we are His very sheep.
Our Good Shepherd's always watching, all day and all night as we sleep.

We're persuaded that nothing can harm us—neither angels, nor death, nor life,
nor powers or principalities that would try to generate strife.

Neither things that are present, or those yet to
come; neither creature, or depth, or height
shall be able to separate us from our Father.
He loves us with all of His might.

God loves us because we're His chosen.
He's adopted us as daughters and sons.
We're pastors, teachers, evangelists, and priests;
we're deacons and elders; we're singers and nuns.

He loved us while we were yet sinners.
True love is what He's magnified.
And through the blood of Jesus Christ,
we've been justified, and sanctified, and glorified!

Learn to trust in Jesus! That's the best advice one can give.
When you trust and lean on Jesus, He'll show you how to live!

Your voice I long to hear ...
Impressions from the Lord, my God!

Sunday: _____

_____

_____

Monday: _____

_____

_____

Tuesday: _____

_____

_____

Wednesday: _____

_____

_____

Thursday: _____

_____

_____

Friday: _____

_____

_____

Saturday: _____

_____

_____

REASON 35—WEEK 35
Deny Ourselves and Follow Christ!
Mark 8:1–38

Take up your cross and follow Christ, but first deny yourself.
Your possessions cannot save you; they'll just occupy space on your shelf.

Do you think that it shall profit you to focus upon worldly gain?
Wealth without Christ is valueless, and leads to an eternity of pain.

Christ gave Himself to save your soul; He valued you so greatly.
Ask yourself this question, my friend: what have you done for Christ lately?

Invite the Lord to spit on your eyes,
and to anoint you with spiritual ears.
Then you'll see and hear your precious Savior;
He'll erase all your doubts and your fears!

Be not ashamed of your Savior. The words that He spoke are still true.
He wants you to boldly declare them to those who are following you.

Christ has proclaimed you as spotless,
whom the sins of this world cannot bother.
Rejoice for the Son of Man's return to the earth
with holy angels sent by His Father.

So deny yourself and follow Christ. Sounds easy, but it's so hard to do.
Feel the pain and separation our Savior suffered through.
And understand just what Jesus did for you!

Your voice I long to hear ...
Impressions from the Lord, my God!

Sunday: _____

_____

Monday: _____

_____

Tuesday: _____

_____

Wednesday: _____

_____

Thursday: _____

_____

_____

Friday: _____

_____

_____

Saturday: _____

_____

_____

REASON 36—WEEK 36
I Trust in You, Lord Jesus!
Proverbs 3

I'll not forsake Your law, my King; I'll follow each and every command.
For length of days, long life, and peace, on Your promises, Lord, I'll stand.

I trust in You, Lord Jesus, as the proven guardian of my soul.
I rest in Your pure love for me; I surrender to You full control.

Whatever this year may bring to me, it first has to come through Your hand.
So, I earnestly cast all my cares upon You as I follow the events You have planned.

You see my future. You see my past. You see everything in between.
All the steps that You would have me take, by You have already been seen.

I will not doubt Your goodness, Lord. My life bears witness of Your love.
You've given me what I don't deserve, things that I could only dream of.

I have no need to worry. You have a plan that I can't see.
And when I trust You fully, You'll perform Your plan in me.

I trust You, Lord, with all my heart; there's no better thing I can do!
I'll lean not on my own understanding, but in all my ways, I'll acknowledge You!

Your voice I long to hear ...
Impressions from the Lord, my God!

Sunday: _____

_____

Monday: _____

_____

Tuesday: _____

_____

Wednesday: _____

_____

Thursday: _____

_____

Friday: _____

_____

Saturday: _____

_____

REASON 37—WEEK 37
Look Straight Ahead Unto Jesus!
Proverbs 4

Moses, as the servant of God, was strong, courageous, and bold.
Joshua, as his replacement, was honored to do all that he'd been told.

We're not to turn to the right or the left, but we
are to look straight ahead unto Jesus.
For He is the One Who atoned for our sins; and
redeemed is how His Father sees us.

We know we have sinned and all fallen short
of the mark that God set before us.
But through Jesus Christ and the blood that He spilled,
we're approved for God's heavenly chorus.

Thank God for His Son, and for what He has done,
and for all of the stripes that He took.
We'll join with the saints in God's heavenly choir,
for our names are inscribed in God's Book!

Don't start to worry and don't start to fret that
you simply just aren't good enough.
For with God, all things are possible, and He's
infused you with just the right stuff.

It's not about you. It's all about Jesus, our Savior, our Lord, and our King.
Don't think about all of the things you can't do,
but with all of your heart and soul, sing!

Rejoice in the Lord! Praise His Holy Name!
Yield to His Spirit that frees us.
Look not to the right, look not to the left, but
look straight ahead unto Jesus!

Your voice I long to hear ...
Impressions from the Lord, my God!

Sunday: _____

_____

_____

Monday: _____

_____

_____

Tuesday: _____

_____

_____

Wednesday: _____

_____

_____

Thursday: _____

_____

_____

Friday: _____

_____

_____

Saturday: _____

_____

_____

Reason 38—Week 38
When You Are Weary, Come to Jesus!
Matthew 11:1–30

When you are tired and weary, when your mind is filled with tension or fear,
bring all your cares to the Master, for the voice of His children He'll hear.

When you feel so alone and forsaken,
by sheer strength you try to pull yourself through.
Do not deceive yourself but receive His strength.
God's love can empower you.

He invites you each day to come to Him.
He understands every struggle you face.
Come sit at the feet of Jesus. Experience His love and His grace.

He was tempted in ways you are tempted. He knows just how hard life can be.
But know, as Lord of the universe, He came to set His people free.

He wants you to know you can trust Him.
He wants you to know He is good.
He cares for you unlike any other. He cares like you wish others could.

Don't travel this road all forsaken. Yield to His way that is best!
Bring all your cares to The Master. In Him, your soul will find rest.

When you are tired and weary, with your mind filled with tension and fear,
leave your cares and your woes with your Master.
And, watch as they all disappear.

Your voice I long to hear ...
Impressions from the Lord, my God!

Sunday: _____

_____

_____

Monday: _____

_____

_____

Tuesday: _____

_____

_____

Wednesday: _____

_____

_____

Thursday: _____

_____

_____

Friday: _____

_____

_____

Saturday: _____

_____

_____

REASON 39—WEEK 39
The First Words That You Speak!
2 Timothy 2

God's Spirit lives within you, and He has called you His elect.
So when you speak to others, be sure of the words you select.

May the first words that you speak help to comfort the weary.
May they uplift the hopeless, and bring a smile to the teary.

Allow the light of the Lord to gloriously shine
when you speak to a friend or a foe.
May the tone of your voice speak volumes in letting
them know Who it is that you know!

Help remove their façade and concerns, and let them know that you care.
Show them you're someone whom they can trust,
as you lift up their problems in prayer!

May your very first words be tender, as you speak with words so sincere.
May the feelings that your words engender,
assure them that Jesus Christ is so near!

May your words be filled with compassion, a passion so true and so real,
that you will astound both the young and the old
when they sense how you truly feel.

May your first words be so gentle, and so easy to understand.
They'll know you've spent time with Jesus;
they'll know He's still holding your hand.

(Pause) What message from God would you feel coming through,
if the first words that you speak were somehow directed toward you?

Your voice I long to hear ...
Impressions from the Lord, my God!

Sunday: _____
_____
_____

Monday: _____
_____
_____

Tuesday: _____
_____
_____

Wednesday: _____
_____
_____

Thursday: _____
_____
_____

Friday: _____
_____
_____

Saturday: _____
_____
_____

God Moments

He is God all by Himself. Express to
Him your heartfelt adoration of His
unfathomable majesty and grace.

Reason 40—Week 40
There's So Much We Don't Know!
Job 38

Our God spoke to His servant, Job, in a whirlwind long ago.
There were so very many things that Job just did not know.

Job could not see the treasures in God's snow or in the hail,
or how God uses all of His creation to help mankind prevail!

Job could not grasp what all of God's creations were made for;
and how our God will always prevail and win any seemingly unwinnable war.

Job just was not able to see and to fathom God's grand plan.
His eyes had not been opened. He was not God; he was just a man.

But our God is our divine Creator. He sits high, sees everything below.
And He knows incomparably so much more than we will ever know!

We are children who, just like Job, fail to see all God is doing.
We live our lives not knowing that we are the treasure God's been pursuing.

God knows each new tomorrow. He sends the lightning, rain, and ice!
He commands, and they come quickly. He need not beckon twice! Yes,
He commands, and they come quickly. He need not call them twice!

Your voice I long to hear ...
Impressions from the Lord, my God!

Sunday: _____

_____

_____

Monday: _____

_____

_____

Tuesday: _____

_____

_____

Wednesday: _____

_____

_____

Thursday: _____

_____

_____

Friday: _____

_____

_____

Saturday: _____

_____

_____

REASON 41—WEEK 41
A House Built for the Lord!
2 Chronicles 2 – 6

King Solomon, he determined to build a house fit for his King!
He'd been commissioned by God to do it, and he desired to do the right thing.

He gathered all the craftsmen. He bought all the right stuff.
To make sure that it pleased His God, he bought more than just enough!

He bought the silver and the jewels. There was so much to behold!
He bought cedar trees and fir trees; overlaid the doors with purest gold!

He made curtains and the tables, the work of skilled masons.
They made pillars, chapiters, gold shovels, and one hundred gold basons.

They worked with such passion as they followed God's plan.
They worked for their Heavenly Father.
They worked for God's appointed man!

As they finished God's new house, and praised Him in one accord,
God's cloud came in and dwelled within the house built for the Lord!

You too have been dedicated as a house built for our King.
He longs to dwell within you. He longs to be your Everything!

Walk in sinless beauty! May God's Word pierce like a sword!
For you have been designed to be a house built for the Lord!

Your voice I long to hear ...
Impressions from the Lord, my God!

Sunday: _____

_____

_____

Monday: _____

_____

_____

Tuesday: _____

_____

_____

Wednesday: _____

_____

_____

Thursday: _____

_____

_____

Friday: _____

_____

_____

Saturday: _____

_____

_____

REASON 42—WEEK 42
Early Will I Seek Thee, My God!
Psalm 63

Early will I seek Thee, Lord, as I raise up from my bed.
You kept me through the midnight hours as I rested my weary head.

My soul does thirst; my flesh does long for You in dry and thirsty lands.
I will bless You while I live, my God; in surrender, I lift up both my hands.

Heavenly Father, You are my God, and this I will declare,
so that no one can truthfully say to You that somehow, they were unaware.

We have felt your awesome love for us; You came and did not tarry.
You've shown Yourself to be our God in our hearts, Your sanctuary.

I will bless You daily while I live, my God. I will praise Your Holy Name!
My soul will daily praise You, Lord God! Your presence burns in me as a flame.

I'll rejoice forever as I reside in the shadow of Your wings.
And may I always please You, Lord, in both the great and lesser things.

The enemy shall not harm me, for You've preserved my soul.
Though I walk through the valley of the shadow
of death, Your love has made me whole!

Your voice I long to hear ...
Impressions from the Lord, my God!

Sunday: _____

_____

Monday: _____

_____

Tuesday: _____

_____

Wednesday: _____

_____

Thursday: _____

_____

Friday: _____

_____

Saturday: _____

_____

_____

REASON 43—WEEK 43
Give Thanks to the Lord!
Psalm 136

Give thanks to the Lord, for He is good, for His mercy endures forever.
He's the God of gods, and the Lord of lords, and His power no one can sever!

Oh, give thanks all ye people to our Good, Good
Lord, for His mercy endures forever!
Give your praise to the One Who is to be
adored, for His mercy endures forever!

Give thanks to the Lord, Who alone does great
wonders, for His mercy endures forever.
Praise Him Who sends forth the lightnings and the
thunders, for His mercy endures forever.

Give thanks to the Lord, Who made the great
lights, for His mercy endures forever.
He made the sun for the days, the stars and moon for
the nights, for His mercy endures forever.

Give thanks to the Lord, Who set Israel free,
for His mercy endures forever.
Give thanks to the God, Who parted the Red
Sea, for His mercy endures forever.

Give thanks to the Lord, Who made the sea stand
as a wall, for His mercy endures forever.
Give thanks to the God, Who in love, delivered
us all, for His mercy endures forever.

No one can snatch you from the hand of God,
not with knife, nor sword, or whatever.
So give thanks to the Lord, for He is good,
for His mercy endures forever!

Your voice I long to hear ...
Impressions from the Lord, my God!

Sunday: _____

_____

_____

Monday: _____

_____

_____

Tuesday: _____

_____

_____

Wednesday: _____

_____

_____

Thursday: _____

_____

_____

Friday: _____

_____

_____

Saturday: _____

_____

_____

REASON 44—WEEK 44
Have You Ever Been in the Lion's Den?
Daniel 6

Have you ever been in the lion's den? Have you ever felt forlorn?
Have you ever felt self-pity, wondered why you'd ever been born?

Well Daniel was a praying man, and he prayed three times each day.
He desired the fellowship of the Lord, His God, to guide him on his way.

But Daniel was placed in trouble because of his daily devotions.
His enemies wanted to fill him with fears and all types of ungodly emotions.

He was placed inside the hungry lion's den, through no fault of his own.
And Daniel knew that God could use the den to make His glory known.

Now King Darius, He loved Daniel, and he fasted all that night.
Rose up early the very next day, hoping Daniel was still alright.

But Daniel knew the Lord His God, and on His Lord relied.
God shut the lions' mouths so tight you'd think they'd all been tied.

When Daniel spoke unto the king, the king was so relieved,
to hear old Daniel praise his God; then the king himself believed!

When you find yourself in the lion's den, just know that God is able
to rescue and deliver you. So, in Him, let your heart be stable!

Your voice I long to hear ...
Impressions from the Lord, my God!

Sunday: _____
_____
_____

Monday: _____
_____
_____

Tuesday: _____
_____
_____

Wednesday: _____
_____
_____

Thursday: _____
_____
_____

Friday: _____
_____
_____

Saturday: _____
_____
_____

REASON 45—WEEK 45
The Kingdom of Heaven Is at Hand!
Matthew 3, 4

The kingdom of heaven is truly at hand; we don't know the day or the hour
when the Lord will return to rule the earth in His beauty and awesome power!

The time to repent is now, my friend. Words that John spoke are so true!
For John came to prepare the way of the Lord, and give us a new point of view!

The day will arrive as a thief in the night. Now is the time to prepare!
Invite Christ to be Lord of your life, lest you be caught unaware!

You won't be alarmed when that day comes if you give Jesus your life today!
Accept Jesus Christ as your Lord and God. There is no easier way!

Now some may think that the deeds they do
will save them from death at that time.
But the good we do are as dirty rags, and will not be worth a thin dime!

Do not trust in the things that you can do, for
you know just how powerless you are.
You need to rely upon the King of all kings! He
positioned and He named every star!

Shall not He who formed everything that we
see, hear the heartfelt cry of His child?
Do it now, my friend; surrender all to Him. Before God, be reconciled!

Your voice I long to hear ...
Impressions from the Lord, my God!

Sunday: _____

_____

Monday: _____

_____

_____

Tuesday: _____

_____

_____

Wednesday: _____

_____

_____

Thursday: _____

_____

_____

Friday: _____

_____

_____

Saturday: _____

_____

REASON 46—WEEK 46
How Will You Answer?
Matthew 27

Jesus was led unto Pilot, who asked, "Are you king of the Jews?"
Jesus said, "Thou sayest," and Pilot knew he'd soon have to choose!

Pilot asked the people, "What shall I do then
with Jesus which is called Christ?"
The crowd wanted Pilot to bear all the blame,
but Pilot would not be so enticed!

And when they shouted, "Crucify Him!" Pilot
asked them, what was Christ's crime?
But the people screamed louder, "Crucify
Him!" time after time after time.

Pilot washed his hands before them; said,
"I am innocent of the blood of this just man."
They said, "May His blood be upon us,"
and thus the Substitution began.

So how will you answer the question
and what will you do with God's Christ?
Will you be inclined to go with the crowd
or today receive God's sacrifice?

Have you been washed in the blood of the Lamb?
Is Jesus your Lord and your friend?
His friends do as they've been commanded,
and we're getting so close to the end!

Today, the choice is yours to make; it's yours and yours alone.
Don't wait, for you will soon give an answer,
as you bow before God's holy throne!

Your voice I long to hear ...
Impressions from the Lord, my God!

Sunday: _____

_____

_____

Monday: _____

_____

_____

Tuesday: _____

_____

_____

Wednesday: _____

_____

_____

Thursday: _____

_____

_____

Friday: _____

_____

_____

Saturday: _____

_____

_____

REASON 47—WEEK 47
God Moments!
Matthew 19

God moments are those quiet times when you're in your secret place
and you enter into worship and snuggle into God's embrace.

As you sit, your mind is peaceful. You can feel the Father's love.
And you know that in eternity, this is what heaven is made of.

Sometimes God remains silent. Sometimes He speaks your name.
But you just want to be with Him. That's the reason why you came.

So rest within this moment; let the Lord infuse your being.
Let Him love you as you love Him back.
Loving your Lord is incredibly freeing!

There's no desire for pretense; every thought and word is real.
Your Father sees your inner heart and knows exactly how you feel.

Just what is a God Moment? It's your encounter with the King,
where He'll replace your sorrow with a song of praise to sing.

What's the purpose of God Moments? That's a question you might ask …
It's to give your all to Almighty God and in His glorious presence bask!

Your voice I long to hear …
Impressions from the Lord, my God!

Sunday: _____

_____

_____

Monday: _____

_____

_____

Tuesday: _____

_____

_____

Wednesday: _____

_____

_____

Thursday: _____

_____

_____

Friday: _____

_____

_____

Saturday: _____

_____

_____

REASON 48—WEEK 48
Don't Give Up! Lift Jesus Up! Higher!
John 12

When it seems that circumstances tend to hamper your desire ...
When even friends and loved ones place a damper on your fire ...

When you feel the world around you is filled
with woe and pain and ire ...
When you want to throw the towel in and sink in the muck and mire ...

Don't listen to the enemy. He's nothing but a liar!
Trust Christ to save your weary soul! He is your Magnifier!

Just listen to The Master's words; they're Words made to inspire.
Trust in the Lord to give you strength. He'll be your Purifier!

Let Him lead you through the wilderness
and watch what will transpire.
He'll help you see God's plan for you; He is your Sanctifier!

Do not give up! Lift Jesus up! It's coming down to the wire.
When you stand before almighty God, He is your Justifier!

So, if you want to know God's ways, then seek Him and inquire
how you may serve the living God, and lift Him higher and higher!

Your voice I long to hear ...
Impressions from the Lord, my God!

Sunday: _____

_____

_____

Monday: _____

_____

_____

Tuesday: _____

_____

_____

Wednesday: _____

_____

_____

Thursday: _____

_____

_____

Friday: _____

_____

_____

Saturday: _____

_____

_____

REASON 49—WEEK 49
I Present to You My Sacrifice!
Romans 12

I present to You my sacrifice, my work, my mind, my soul!
I give them to You freely, Lord! I surrender full control!

I lay before You, Jesus, this work You had me do.
I did not do it just for me, but also for You too!

This task You gave to me, Lord God, has been a pleasurable ride.
I've learned much more than I can tell; You placed so much inside!

I thank You, Lord, for trusting me with a job that I've adored,
for I have penned the words You wrote. All glory to You, Lord!

It was not me who started it, but Your Spirit bid me come.
And so I started writing; I know where all the words came from!

I'll not conform unto this world as You transform my mind.
And gleefully I will follow You, keeping always one step behind!

My Lord, I pray this pleases You! Thank You for being my Guide!
May those who read rejoice to be Your
beloved, Your church, Your bride!

Your voice I long to hear ...
Impressions from the Lord, my God!

Sunday: _____
_____
_____

Monday: _____
_____

Tuesday: _____
_____
_____

Wednesday: _____
_____

Thursday: _____
_____

Friday: _____
_____

Saturday: _____
_____
_____

REASON 50—WEEK 50
The Story of Christmas Is Love!
Luke 2

The angel said to the shepherds, "Fear not, I bring tidings of joy!"
In love, your Father's redeemed you, in the form of a baby boy!

The story of Christmas is all about love, seeing things through a heavenly eye.
For God gave His Only Begotten Son to save us, so that we would not die.

The story of Christmas is Jesus, the Christ, the Messiah, God's Son;
of how He gave Himself away, to join us with His Father, as one.

The story of Christmas is spending.
Spending time with the ones we hold dear;
spending precious moments in solemn prayer,
sending kisses and hugs and good cheer.

While Christ was here, He knew that His task
was to seek and to save all the lost.
He offered His life, the perfect sacrifice;
He paid the debt that all our sins cost.

He taught us, and caught us, and brought us to
Himself, so that we might learn what is true.
He sought us as men search for riches and fame.
Christ did what no other would do.

So, when you think about Christmas,
and give thanks to your Father above,
just know that you're dear, for God's Word makes
it clear, that the story of Christmas is Love!

Your voice I long to hear ...
Impressions from the Lord, my God!

Sunday: _____

_____

_____

Monday: _____

_____

_____

Tuesday: _____

_____

_____

Wednesday: _____

_____

_____

Thursday: _____

_____

_____

Friday: _____

_____

_____

Saturday: _____

_____

_____

Reason 51—Week 51
Lord Jesus, You Took My Blame!
John 1

To show Your Father's love for us is the reason that You came.
As the very precious Lamb of God, You took away my blame.

Lord Jesus, I wish that I could describe the greatness of Your love.
If I used a million, billion words, I would still be guilty of

Understating Your infinite worth, for I cannot comprehend
how You love us so steadfastly, with a love that will not end.

My blameless God, my blameless King, what You did seemed so absurd,
to give Your precious life for those who would not obey Your Word!

I cannot understand it, but I receive it. I know that it is true!
That You are always loving us in all You say and do!

My words seem so inadequate, so, Lord, please help me to write
words that convict but not condemn, to guide us to Your light.

You loved us through our sin, dear Lord. You loved us through our shame.
For all the wrongs that we've done, Lord, You chose to take our blame!

Your voice I long to hear ...
Impressions from the Lord, my God!

Sunday: _____

_____

_____

Monday: _____

_____

_____

Tuesday: _____

_____

_____

Wednesday: _____

_____

_____

Thursday: _____

_____

_____

Friday: _____

_____

_____

Saturday: _____

_____

_____

REASON 52—WEEK 52
Near the End with Jesus Christ in Mind!
Looking unto Jesus, the Author and Finisher ...
Hebrews 12, 13

We're at the end of another year! Lord, You've been so kind!
We believe, in faith, we'll make it to the end with Christ in mind!

This year is just about over; almost time to say, "Adieu."
We take the time to thank You, Father, for blessings given us by You!

Yes, it's time to thank You, Jesus, for love and blessings without number,
for beauty of the daytime skies, for peaceful nights of slumber!

Thank You, Holy Spirit, for comfort and presence that's so pure.
As we listen to Your whispers, You lead us
through pastures green and secure!

Oh, the clothes we wore, and the foods we ate,
and the times we laughed and played.
And the times of peace and stillness, Lord,
when to You, our God, we prayed!

There were days we knew we needed You.
There were days we felt so strong.
And, all the while, You provided for us, and
showed us right from wrong.

As You close the chapter on this year, Lord, and begin a brand-new one,
we thank You, Father, we receive You, Holy Spirit!
We praise You, Jesus Christ, God's Son!

Your voice I long to hear ...
Impressions from the Lord, my God!

Sunday: _____
_____
_____

Monday: _____
_____
_____

Tuesday: _____
_____
_____

Wednesday: _____
_____
_____

Thursday: _____
_____
_____

Friday: _____
_____
_____

Saturday: _____
_____
_____

Noteworthy Remembrances from the Lord ...

_____

_____

_____

_____

_____

_____

_____

_____

_____

_____

_____

_____

_____

_____

_____

_____

_____

_____

_____

Thank you sincerely for taking this journey with me.

- I pray that you found some joy in the journey.
- I pray that you were able to draw nearer unto God as you reflected on our Lord and Savior, Jesus Christ.
- I pray that you were in some way reminded of the price that God paid in order to give you and me the gift of eternal life.
- I pray that each impression you received, each scripture, each picture, each little poem, and each phrase pointed you to our divine Creator!
- And, above all, please remember that God, our heavenly Father, the Creator of the universe, used a human vessel to pen the words, and that (1) He alone is the author of this little book, (2) He loves you with a sincere and perfect love, (3) He longs to fellowship with you every day, and (4) He has paved the way for you and me to spend all of eternity with Him!

A Little Bit about the Human Author

Hi. I am the author, and this is my brief story.
It's filled with some sadness; it's replete with God's glory.

It's filled with God's love, so abundant, so clear.
Even through my rebellion, God showed Himself near.

I was born way out east, a lovely city called Chester,
with a gap in my heart that seemed to grow and to fester.

I learned at age four that no one knew my mother,
nor father, nor sister, nor kinfolk, nor brother.

So, at age four, I decided, "Life just isn't fair!"
I wanted someone to love me. I needed someone to care.

Though I felt so all alone, I learned how to survive.
Then things really got crazy by the time I turned five!

Some people moved in who knew so much about living.
They knew lots about taking, not as much about giving.

They taught me some things I did not want to learn.
They knew when to be gentle; they knew how to be stern.

I really tried to forget all the things that we'd done!
I just wanted to play, to have friends, to have fun!

I even prayed God would take away what I knew.
For I was but a child, and wanted "child things" to do.

But God chose not to remove the things I'd been taught,
the things I'd been through, or the things that life brought.

For God's grace was sufficient, as I was later to know.
God's love never left me, but past thoughts would not go.

I clearly questioned, and could not understand,
how bad things could happen to a child in God's hand.

But this world, it is fallen, and one day it will end.
And my God had a plan I could not comprehend.

Why had people made choices to do such and such?
Why had they listened to voices that were so out of touch?

But my task was to serve God in faith, day by day,
to hear His soft voice whisper, "This is the way."

To know He was with me through all that occurred,
to follow Him always, with steps undeterred.

He understood all my pain, comprehended my sorrow.
Saw my past, saw my present, and He planned my tomorrow.

God knew there'd be debts that I would have to pay
for choices I would make as I traveled life's way.

I couldn't blame anyone for the deeds that I did.
I'd hoped my good deeds would somehow keep them all hid.

But good deeds were not able to erase all my wrong,
though I cried as I sang an old Dallas Holm song.

"I will rise again," I sang with such feeling.
But deep in my heart, I still needed healing.

I still had not changed and become God's new man.
So, God, in His love, wove phase two of His plan.

He sent me the insight to see what I'd become,
And revealed to me just what He'd delivered me from.

And I grew tired of sinning, living just for myself.
I wanted to permanently put my old man on a shelf.

So, I sang, "Change my heart, oh God," and this time I meant it.
My God knew that I wanted salvation and sent it!

The phone call came on a Friday at noon.
As the officer spoke, my head started to swoon.

I listened intently and heard all he'd said.
My sins were uncovered, risen up from the dead.

My life as I knew it was about to be changed.
My family, my church, were forever estranged.

The pain and the grief that bombarded my life
cut me like the sharp blade of a serrated knife.

The pain that I caused had caught up with me now.
When I'd sung, "Change my heart," the Lord had answered my vow.

The prison walls beckoned me; I was sent away.
The Lord had answered me, and I had to obey.

In His mercy, He'd saved me; He'd given me a new life.
Though many times there are still struggles,
and many times there's still strife.

I can humbly proclaim that my debts have been paid,
for wrong deeds that I've done, for bad choices I've made.

But my time in the wilderness was just a down payment.
God began, in His mercy, to clothe me with new raiment.

For Christ paid for my sins; He covered me with His Grace,
on that old rugged cross, when He died in my place.

He arose three days later, as God's spotless Lamb,
to proclaim me as holy before the Great I Am!

And God's given this lesson about which there's no doubt:
when we choose to sin, our sins will be found out!

So now I sing, "Hallelujah," with all the fervor within me,
for just as God has promised, His truth has set me free!

From your brother in the Lord,

Anthony

The author wrote the words during his quiet God Moments. The work is intended to express his love for his Creator and his thankfulness for the finished work of Jesus Christ on the cross at Calvary.

He resides in Michigan, and this is his first attempt at publishing a book.

Printed in the United States
By Bookmasters